SEE AMERICAN HISTORY

THE WILD WEST

1804–1890

★

The Art of

MORT KÜNSTLER

Text by

JAMES I. ROBERTSON, JR.

★

ABBEVILLE KIDS

A DIVISION OF ABBEVILLE PRESS

New York   London

*In memory of Lou Oshins, my football coach
at Brooklyn College and lifelong friend, who nurtured
my interest in history. —MK*

Front and back cover: The Oklahoma land rush. See page 42.
Frontispiece: Sioux Indians dressed for battle. See page 20.
Back endpaper: The hard journey west. See page 18.

Editor: Nicole Lanctot
Designer: Misha Beletsky
Composition: Ada Rodriguez
Production manager: Louise Kurtz

First edition
1 3 5 7 9 10 8 6 4 2

ISBN 978-0-7892-1260-3

Library of Congress Cataloging-in-Publication Data available upon request

For bulk or premium sales and for text adoption procedures, write to Customer Service Manager, 116 West 23rd Street, New York, NY 10011, or call 1-800-ARTBOOK.
Visit Abbeville Press online at www.abbeville.com.

TABLE OF CONTENTS

The Story of the Wild West

Cowboys, American Indians, horses, buffalo, roaming gunfighters, wagon trains, and the world's longest railroad — these are some of the images that may come to mind when you think of the Wild West. But they are only part of the long history of the land west of the Mississippi River.

For thousands of years, the only inhabitants of North America were Native Americans. They lived in groups known as tribes, or bands, and each tribe had its own language, customs, and territory. Apaches were cave-dwellers in the deserts of the Southwest; Great Plains Indians roamed over the huge barren flatlands between the great Mississippi River and the Rocky Mountains; and the Haida lived on islands off the coast of the Pacific Northwest.

Around 1492, Spanish explorers became the first Europeans to set foot in the North American wilderness. They brought with them muskets and metal armor, as well as their religion and language. Next came European fur-trappers hunting for beaver, otter, and wolves. While many of these explorers and trappers traveled alone, they established trails that would become highways during a period of great migration.

The Spaniards also brought with them an animal that was vital to settlement of the West: the horse. Frontiersmen became totally dependent on the horse as a means of transportation. In fact, horses were considered so valuable during the time of the Wild West that stealing one was punishable by death!

With the discovery of gold in California in 1848, rumors ran wild of streets paved in the precious metal. Tens of thousands of people headed west in the Gold Rush, hoping to strike it rich. Within two years, the mostly unexplored territory of California had become an official state.

The American Civil War (from 1861 to 1865) did not stop the flow of migration. In fact, an act passed by Congress during the war years was designed to encourage those who were thinking of heading west.

In 1865, the Great West was a huge wilderness area covering around two million square miles. It contained plains, mountains, deserts, and forests. Some of the forests were so dense it was said that a squirrel could jump from tree to tree for hundreds of miles without ever touching the ground!

By 1900, the entire region had been carved into ten states and four territories. Never before in history had so large an area been settled so quickly.

Hundreds of wagon trains loaded with American and European pioneers and their meager belongings snaked slowly westward. Some were looking for better farmland or simply for land of their own. Others headed west because they had broken the law and wanted a fresh start. Nothing in life was easy for the pioneers. Danger was present every mile of the way: extreme weather, hostile tribes, stampeding buffalo, wild animals, lack of water, sickness, a broken wagon wheel, getting lost.... The journey was as much a battle for survival as it was a pilgrimage to a better home. As one pioneer woman wrote in her diary:

> The last of the Black Hills we crossed this afternoon, over the roughest and most desolate piece of ground that was ever made (called by some the Devil's Crater). Not a drop of water, nor a spear of grass to be seen, nothing but barren hills, bare broken rock, sand and dust.

With the arrival of the railroad, travel became much easier. Now, the "Iron Horse" tamed the wilderness, allowing people to move faster, more safely, and in all kinds of weather. The completion of the transcontinental line in 1869, which connected the Atlantic and the Pacific coasts, saw the number of pioneers soar to record levels.

Two main obstacles stood in the way of Western settlement: Native Americans and buffalo. Eventually, pioneers and soldiers conquered the first group and slaughtered the other to the point of extinction.

With the taming of the Wild West came lawlessness. Pioneers had staked their lives on land claims, herds of livestock, and possible sources of gold, and they had a lot to lose. Some of the first frontier towns — Deadwood, Abilene, Tucson, Dodge City, Tombstone — were infamous for gambling halls and murders. Legendary gunslingers, famous sheriffs, shoot-outs between good guys and bad, all were part of this stage of development. (While some of the stories are true, many are not.)

It took more than 25 years to bring law and order to the Wild West. During that time, government officials regularly made and then broke treaties with Native Americans. When U.S. cavalry attacked a tribe, soldiers often killed not only the men but also the women and children.

In 1890, the U.S. Census Bureau announced that there was no new land left to settle in the western frontier, and so the Old West was officially dead. However, proof of the pioneers' hard work and determination is everywhere in the towns and cities they helped build.

The Land Lies Waiting

Long before Europeans appeared in North America, Native American tribes of every description inhabited the West.

The Paiute (ABOVE RIGHT) and the Pueblo lived in the Southwest. They were expert farmers, growing crops of squash, beans, corn, and cotton. They also raised turkeys and used spears and traps to hunt deer and other wild animals. Little clothing was required because of the desert heat.

The Haida (RIGHT) made their home on islands in the Pacific Northwest. They were skilled fishermen, using hooks, nets, and spears to catch fish and seals—and even whales! Tall, beautifully carved totem poles made from cedar logs decorated many Haida villages and homes. The figures carved on the poles represented the totems (animals or mythological creatures) from which a family traced its origin.

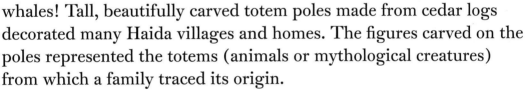

The largest inhabitants of the Wild West, both in size and in number, were the buffalo (LEFT). The Great Plains Indians depended on these huge shaggy creatures for survival. Every part of the buffalo was used. Their flesh was food, their hides became clothing and shelters, their bones were fashioned into tools, and their dried droppings (known as "buffalo chips") were burned as fuel.

Some 30 million buffalo grazed on the Plains at the end of the Civil War. Then, because of the coming of the railroad and wars with American Indians unwilling to give up their rightful lands, settlers and soldiers began killing buffalo in great numbers.

First Explorers

★1540–1550

Spanish explorers were the first Europeans to arrive in the West. In the years 1400 to 1700, these conquistadores (conquerors) went all over the world. They laid claim to territories and opened trade routes that would speed settlement.

In 1540, Francisco Vázquez de Coronado led an expedition from Mexico through Arizona. The men were searching for the fabled City of Cibola, said to contain huge quantities of gold. Coronado's group split up into two parties, and Coronado did not travel with the party that reached the Grand Canyon.

However, when one group reached the Grand Canyon and were unable to cross the wide chasms, they returned to Mexico empty-handed.

These Spanish expeditions introduced horses, mules, guns, and metal armor to the New World, along with superior military knowledge. Any Native American tribe that stood in their way, such as the Apache in Mexico and Arizona, received harsh treatment. The Spanish also introduced diseases like smallpox and typhoid fever, which Native Americans had never known. For this reason, they had no resistance to the diseases and died in great numbers.

The Apache quickly saw the value of the horses the Spanish had brought and became the best horsemen of any American Indian tribe. Because the Apache looked after their animals so well, their horses could travel up to 100 miles a day.

In this painting (BELOW), notice the well-fed brown horse that the lead Apache is riding. It contrasts sharply with the underfed wild horses that are being herded through a mountain pass.

Staking Claims

★1500–1770

A herd of buffalo was not only the source of that day's food but also provided the essentials of life in the months ahead, and so Native Americans never killed more buffalo than they needed. In a hunt, they would choose the largest and the lamest of the buffalo for that day's targets (ABOVE).

In 1769, Gaspar de Portolá (RIGHT, on horseback with the spyglass) served as governor of New Spain, as California was then called. He

had founded Catholic missions (religious settlements) in San Diego, Monterey, and other places along the coast. Learning that a Russian expedition was coming south from Alaska, Portolá organized a party and headed north. With him were 63 soldiers on horseback, armed with muskets and spears. One hundred mules carried supplies, while two Franciscan monks traveled with the group to establish missions on whatever land was claimed.

Portolá (BELOW) halted when he reached the top of a hill and discovered a huge bay on the other side. He named the area Point San Pedro. Finding no Russians, Portolá began the 600-mile journey home, but illness swept through the group, and when provisions ran out, the men were forced to eat some of their mules.

Portolá's discovery marked the birth of a city that would later be called San Francisco.

Lewis and Clark Expedition

★1804–1805

In 1803, President Thomas Jefferson bought a huge expanse of land from France. It was almost a million square miles and doubled the size of what was then known as the United States. Jefferson was anxious to know just what the "Louisiana Purchase" contained. So he chose two friends, Meriwether Lewis and William Clark (ABOVE, with map and spyglass), to lead an expedition west, from the Mississippi River to the Pacific coast. The expedition, which began in May 1804 and ended in December 1805, has been called "America's greatest adventure story."

The 40-man party was to map the best waterways to the ocean and study minerals, plants and animals, and weather conditions. A special assignment was to become acquainted with Native American languages and customs. The "Corps of Discovery" expedition across half a continent of unchartered wilderness was filled with danger, mystery, and courage. After traveling 2,000 miles, Clark scribbled in his journal: "Ocean in view! O! the joy." The first well-documented connection between the Atlantic and Pacific oceans had been made.

Often overlooked in those early years of exploration were the fur-trappers. Searching for beaver, otter, and wolves, trappers usually traveled alone (BELOW). The work these "Mountain Men" did was dirty and dangerous. However, the trails they carved out and the maps they drew opened the way for the thousands of pioneers who came later.

Massacre at the Alamo

★1836

All through the 1820s, pioneers set down homesteads in the fertile lands of Mexican-held Texas. By 1835, there were so many new settlements that Texans declared their independence from Mexico. The Mexican president, General Santa Anna, marched north with 1,500 soldiers to put down the rebellion.

At San Antonio, around 250 men barricaded themselves inside an old Franciscan mission called the Alamo. Among the group were famous frontiersmen Jim Bowie and Davy Crockett. Mexican soldiers

laid siege to the mission for 13 days. Inside, the men slowly ran out of ammunition and food. They would have to surrender eventually.

However, Santa Anna refused to wait. At sunrise on March 5, 1836, he ordered his soldiers to storm the Alamo (ABOVE). By the time the battle was over, nearly everyone inside had been killed, and Santa Anna had lost 600 men.

Six weeks later, at the battle of San Jacinto, Texas, Americans inflicted a stunning defeat on Santa Anna's army. The Americans' battle cry? "Remember the Alamo!"

Texas remained a somewhat independent land (claimed by both countries) until 1845, when the American government officially accepted it as a new state. This led to war with Mexico a year later.

The Long Journey

★1840s–1860s

The promise of a new and better life led to thousands of American and European families moving west—first in a stream, and then a flood. Before pioneers could begin their journey, they had to buy a wagon and the horses, mules, or oxen to pull it, pack it with supplies, and join a wagon train. Traveling with a wagon train offered better protection from robbers and attacks by Native Americans, as well as help in case of a breakdown. Wagon trains could be a mile long.

The covered wagons that carried the pioneers in these paintings became known as prairie schooners, or ships of the plains, because their canvas tops billowed in the wind like the sails of a ship.

Wagon trains (BELOW) faced obstacles every mile of the way. Weather ranged from thunderstorms to snowstorms, and from scorching heat to frigid cold. Lack of water and food, river crossings, mountainous terrain, and breakdown of equipment were just a few of the challenges. For many of the pioneers, the most difficult part of their new life was the journey there.

At the end of the day, wagons were arranged in a circle, forming a makeshift corral inside which horses and other livestock could graze and rest. Women, like the one in this painting (LEFT), prepared supper, which was usually potatoes, biscuits, beans, and very salty bacon.

Life on the Plains

★1850–1860

These paintings highlight the two great hazards the European and American pioneers faced in crossing the Great Plains: buffalo and American Indians.

In the first scene (RIGHT), Crow Indians are taking part in a dramatic and deadly movement known as "splitting the herd." Two lines of Crow on horseback attack the buffalo from opposite directions. They ride quickly in a circle that grows smaller and smaller. The first one killed is a great bull. Panic-stricken buffalo gallop in every direction. The Crow then fire arrows or use spears on individual targets.

Buffalo stampeded easily. Notice in the left background that one animal has been knocked head over heels in the rush. When stampeding, these huge, heavy creatures were extremely unpredictable and dangerous.

Naturally, Native Americans resisted the attempts made to steal the lands that had been theirs for thousands of years. Sometimes, they would sign treaties with the U.S. government, agreeing to move to a different area. More often than not, however, the government didn't keep its word, and the Native Americans were forced off that land, too.

Northern Plains Indians were a proud people. When a tribe was threatened, warriors dressed for battle (LEFT). They fought desperately because their land and their way of life were at stake.

Gold!

★1848

On January 24, 1848, James Marshall (LEFT) and John Sutter discovered gold on a fork of the American River in California. There was no way to keep their discovery a secret. Soon, men from all walks of life rushed westward. One observer noted: "All were off for the mines, some on horses, some on carts, and some on crutches."

Forty percent of the soldiers in California deserted to hunt for gold. In less than a year, 75,000 men swooped down on the land. They became known as "Forty-niners" for that coming year, 1849.

From 1849 to 1853, more than 300,000 prospectors descended on gold country. They eventually mined 750,000 pounds of the precious metal, which would be worth around $30 billion today.

Prospecting was generally done on an individual basis (ABOVE). Gold-seekers recognized no law, and all were heavily armed and quick to shoot if they felt their claims were being threatened. One in every twelve miners was murdered.

This period also marked the beginning of a mass extermination, with thousands of Native Americans being massacred in the effort to remove them from California.

California went from wilderness to statehood in just two years. It has been known ever since as the "Golden State."

Delivering the Goods

★1858–1861

The first passenger service through the wide expanse of the Old West was John Butterfield's Overland Stage Company. The line ran for 2,795 miles, from St. Louis to San Francisco. It took a southerly route across Texas and New Mexico to avoid the harsh winter weather and Rocky Mountains to the north. The full trip took 25 days.

Butterfield's means of transportation was a unique coach. "Stage" was the word used for the distance between two stations. Passenger wagons traveled in stages. Hence, they were called "stagecoaches." The Concord (LEFT) was the most popular of the 40 different types of carriages and wagons that Butterfield designed. It

was a six-passenger coach built high and wide to handle the rough trails. Instead of metal springs, the Concord had leather straps for suspension, which caused it to rock back and forth as it traveled. This led the famous writer Mark Twain to liken a stagecoach ride to "a cradle on wheels."

For several years, Pony Express riders (ABOVE) galloped from town

to town with saddlebags full of mail. Settlers sometimes used heavy wagons pulled by slow but strong mules (LEFT) to get goods to remote places. Traveling in a mule train was always dangerous because Native Americans on fast horses could quickly surround it.

Fighting for the Union

★1861

The Civil War swept over the nation in 1861 and threatened the future of such jumping-off places for western settlement as New Orleans, Vicksburg, Memphis, and St. Louis. Whether the frontier state of Missouri would be Union or Confederate was a major issue.

An uneasy, three-month truce existed among the Missourians. Then, a ragtag force of 11,000 untested and undisciplined Southerners gathered in the southwestern part of the state. Strong-willed Union General Nathaniel Lyon, with a force half that size, marched across the state to confront the Confederates.

On August 10, 1861, the two groups met in an intense fight at Wilson's Creek. It was the first large battle west of the Mississippi

River. Confusion marked most of the fight. Lyon was killed, and a Southern counterattack won the day.

Pictured here (LEFT) is Confederate Colonel John McIntosh leading a Louisiana regiment into the action. The colonel was killed early in the charge. Each side suffered about 1,200 casualties, and Missouri remained divided throughout the four-year Civil War.

Farther west (ABOVE), Confederate patrols searched for horses and supplies, while government troops searched for Confederates. Small battles occurred at Valverde and Glorieta Pass in New Mexico.

The Homestead Act

★1862

In the midst of a war that was tearing the nation in two, the federal government opened a door of opportunity for people wanting a new life in the West. In May 1862, Congress passed the Homestead Act.

Up until then, pioneers had to pay the government for the land they settled. Now, the Homestead Act made it much easier for people who had big dreams but few dollars. For a $10 registration fee, people could get 160 acres of unoccupied land west of the Mississippi River and east of the Rocky Mountains. They would gain permanent possession of the land if they lived on it for five years and made improvements to it.

By the end of the Civil War, 25,000 settlers had staked claims to more than three million acres. Ultimately, 500,000 settlers purchased 80 million acres of what had been vast open spaces. Many settlers built their homes from sod (grass and dirt) or constructed dugouts for living space (LEFT). They were commonly called "sodbusters."

The Homestead Act never measured up to its starry-eyed proposal. The law was poorly enforced and widely abused. Many settlers found 160 acres of barren prairie insufficient for farming or ranching. However, cutting and bringing back a Christmas tree for a new home was a thrill (ABOVE).

The Golden Spike

★1869

The construction of a transcontinental railroad was one of America's greatest achievements. The Union Pacific line began laying track westward from Omaha, Nebraska, in 1863. At the same time, the Central Pacific started work on an eastbound line from Sacramento, California.

The exciting goal of linking the two lines together hid a darker side of the project. Corrupt politicians oversaw construction at every level, and tens of millions of dollars in bribes and kickbacks lay underneath the hard work. The Central Pacific used mostly Chinese laborers. Union Pacific workers included a large number of draft dodgers and wanted criminals. Temporary, rowdy camps were taken by rail from point to point and became known as "Hell on Wheels."

The two railway lines were built almost entirely by hand. In the rugged Rocky Mountains, some days only a foot of roadbed could be carved out. On the Great Plains, where the land was mostly flat, Union Pacific laborers were able to lay up to eight miles of track a day.

On May 10, 1869, after six years of construction covering 1,907 miles, the lines merged at Promontory Summit, Utah. The "Golden Spike" (LEFT) was hammered in, uniting the two railroads. The days of the stagecoach were soon over.

On the Open Range

★1830s–1880s

As many as three million wild horses roamed through the foothills and over the prairies of the West. To a settler, they were as necessary to life as food. Roundups (BELOW) occurred every season. Once captured, a horse had to be "broken"—made accustomed to a saddle and rider—and trained. Thereafter, they were the cowboy's closest friend.

In a cattle drive, around 1,500 to 2,000 animals were herded from a ranch to a "cow town," where the cattle were sold. Between 12 and 18 herders were needed. As you can see in these paintings, the cowboy's basic equipment was two blankets and a change of clothing, leather leggings ("chaps"), and a lasso. He wore a pistol on a belt, which also held cartridges, and carried a carbine (a short, light rifle) in a saddle holster. A wide-brimmed hat protected the cowboy from sun and rain.

Bad weather was the worst danger of all on a trail herd. Dust storms limited vision and made breathing difficult. An early snow (BELOW RIGHT) might fall, making it impossible for the cattle to find the grass they needed. A bolt of lightning (RIGHT) could send a nervous herd into a stampede.

Western Law

★1860s–1890s

Books, movies, and television shows have painted a romanticized but often false picture of life in the Wild West. Society was violent. So was justice.

A town's sheriff was the meanest man in town. (Many sheriffs, like the Earp brothers, were former outlaws.) The town marshal did not risk his life in a shoot-out with the "bad guy" in the middle of Main Street. The favorite kind of showdown was actually an ambush — shooting someone from a hiding place and without warning. Former lawman "Wild Bill" Hickok was shot in the back of the head while playing poker.

In this painting (LEFT), a sheriff is taking a man with a shoulder wound to jail. No court system existed in the West. Justice was local, and it was swift. A man condemned to death for a crime might be hanged the same day.

The weapons that men carried came in all shapes and sizes (BELOW). The most popular gun was the 44-caliber, six-shot revolver. It was heavy and quite difficult to fire. Contrary to popular belief, "gunslingers" were not good marksmen, and so when one began shooting, everyone in the area ran for cover.

Buffalo Hunters and Buffalo Soldiers

★1865

American Indians from Montana to Texas followed the tracks of the buffalo herds. The Plains Indians lived in tepees, which were tentlike structures made from cloth or buffalo skins. They were easy to take down and pack up when the time came to follow the wandering herds.

Tribes such as the Sioux, Crow, Kiowa, and Comanche took very good care of their horses. Their livelihood depended on it. Short bows were used when buffalo-hunting, making it easier to shoot arrows from horseback.

In battle against settlers and soldiers, most Native American tribes employed ambush or hit-and-run tactics. They might begin an assault with a loud war cry. Can you hear it in this painting (BELOW)?

In the post–Civil War years, the army recruited men for Western frontier duty, including the men that made up the six African American regiments (RIGHT). The Cheyenne labeled them "buffalo soldiers." The soldiers performed well in spite of racial discrimination and the refusal of some army officers to command them.

Custer's Biggest Mistake

★1876

George Custer was never as good a cavalry commander as he thought he was. In fact, in his West Point class of 1861, he had ranked dead last. Custer conducted himself well enough in the first years of the Civil War to be promoted from captain to brigadier general in the Union Army. He was then 21. But the war ended, and Custer was ordered to return to his rank of captain in the Regular Army.

This gallant but overconfident officer with flashy uniforms wanted his general's stars restored, and so he went west, seeking fame and glory in the fight against Native Americans. Custer became known for his reckless and murderous tactics, but his foolhardy actions came to an end at the Little Bighorn River in eastern Montana.

On June 25, 1876, Custer and his men separated into three groups in preparation for an attack on a large Native American force. Custer had been ordered to wait for reinforcements before telling his men to charge. The headstrong Custer ignored his orders and took one group to launch an attack against what he thought were 500 or so Native Americans. Suddenly, some 2,000 Cheyenne, Sioux, and Arapaho warriors overwhelmed Custer and his cavalrymen. The only survivor in Custer's 220-man force was a horse.

In this painting, Custer (TOP LEFT) is not wearing a hat. He holds a pistol and is standing by the American flag. Can you spot him?

The Native Americans retreated from the area two days later, when the troops Custer had been ordered to wait for arrived.

Passing of an Age
★1870s–1890

In the 1870s, a worldwide demand for buffalo hides increased the slaughter. This in turn sent desperate Native Americans on the warpath. For 15 years after Custer's defeat at the Little Big Horn, soldiers and civilians waged war against the tribes.

The Native Americans could not match the white men in numbers, weapons, or military skills. One by one, the tribes were beaten into submission. A particularly sad case involved the Nez Perce tribe, when government officials broke a treaty and sought to drive them from their ancestral lands in Oregon.

Chief Joseph (ABOVE) of the Nez Perce then led 650 members of his tribe in an attempt to reach the safety of Canada. The pursuing cavalry outnumbered them 16 to 1, yet Chief Joseph's skillful moves time and again prevented capture. On October 5, 1877, after five days in freezing weather, with no blankets or food, Chief Joseph surrendered. To the soldiers he said: "From where the sun now stands, I will fight no more." He had journeyed 1,300 miles and was only a day's march from Canada.

By 1890, the Indian Wars were over.

Until his death in 1904, Chief Joseph lived far from home on a reservation in Idaho. The physician listed his cause of death as "a broken heart."

The Great Land Rush

★1889

In 1838 and 1839, 16,000 Cherokee were forced to leave their homeland for Oklahoma. At least 2,000 of them died along the way. At the end of their "Trail of Tears" were two million acres of barren land designated as the Indian Territory. The Cherokee and other tribes lived there in uncertainty for 50 years. Then, they were shoved aside again, when the federal government decided to open the whole expanse to settlers.

On April 22, 1889, some 55,000 people waited impatiently at the borders of the Indian Territory for the starting time for land-claiming. At noon, cannon boomed, pistols fired, bugles blared, and people in wagons, on horseback, and on foot rushed across the borders to stake a claim, as you can see in this painting. A flood of settlers descended on the land. More than 11,000 claims were filed the first day. A rail line ran north–south through the territory. Two small stops, Oklahoma City and Guthrie, existed that morning. By nightfall, each town had 10,000 residents, with new streets planned and building construction set to begin.

The number of land claims was so huge that three years later, over 5,000 claims were still being contested in court.

The Wild West was no longer wild.

★ The Wild West: Timeline

1540
February 23: Coronado makes an expedition to Arizona.

1769
November 4: Portolá's California expedition discovers San Francisco Bay.

1803
April 30: The United States acquires Louisiana Purchase from France.

1804
May 14: Lewis and Clark set off on their historic expedition.

1836
February 23–March 6: Battle of the Alamo.

April 21: Texans win a decisive victory over Mexican forces at San Jacinto.

1845
December 29: Texas becomes a state.

1848
January 24: Gold is discovered in California.

February 2: The Treaty of Guadalupe Hidalgo ends the Mexican War.

1850
September 9: California becomes a state.

1859
February 14: Oregon becomes a state.

1861
January 29: Kansas becomes a state.

1862
May 20: The Homestead Act is passed.

July 1: The Pacific Railroad Act is passed.

1864
October 31: Nevada becomes a state.

November 29: U.S. troops massacre Cheyenne and Arapaho at Sand Creek, Colorado.

1867
March 1: Nebraska becomes a state.

1868
November 27: Custer's troops massacre Cheyenne at Washita River, Oklahoma Territory.

1869
May 10: The transcontinental railroad is completed at Promontory Summit, Utah.

1876
June 25: Battle of the Little Bighorn, Montana.

August 1: Colorado becomes a state.

1877
October 5: Chief Joseph and his Nez Perce tribe surrender.

1886
September 4: Apache chief Geronimo is the last Native American leader to surrender to U.S. government troops.

1889

November 2: North Dakota and South Dakota become states.

November 8: Montana becomes a state.

November 11: Washington becomes a state.

1890

July 3: Idaho becomes a state.

July 10: Wyoming becomes a state.

December 29: U.S. troops massacre Lakota at Wounded Knee, South Dakota.

1896

January 4: Utah becomes a state.

1907

November 16: Oklahoma becomes a state.

1912

January 6: New Mexico becomes a state.

February 14: Arizona becomes a state.

★ Key People

Bowie, James (1796–1836) A legendary frontiersman and fighter, he was killed at the Alamo. A type of huge knife bears his name today.

Bridger, Jim (1804–1881) The most famous of the fur trappers, he was the first white man to see Yellowstone and the Great Salt Lake.

Butterfield, John Warren (1801–1869) He operated the largest passenger and freight line in the West. Warren also founded companies that would later be known as American Express and Wells Fargo.

Clark, William (1770–1838) A Kentucky planter and co-leader of the Lewis and Clark expedition, he was later a successful soldier and governor.

Cochise (1805–1874) He was the leader of the Chiricahua Apache. For 10 years his warriors conducted raids in the Southwest.

Cody, William (1846–1917) A Pony Express rider, army scout, and star of a long-running rodeo show, he was known as "Buffalo Bill." He admitted to killing 4,282 buffalo in an 18-month period.

Coronado, Francisco Vázquez de (1510–1554) A Spanish general. In 1540 his expedition discovered the Grand Canyon in Arizona.

Crockett, David (1786–1836) He was a folk hero often called "King of the Wild Frontier." He died in the Alamo fighting.

Custer, George Armstrong (1839–1876)
He was an American colonel killed
in the battle of the Little Bighorn.
Military officials were openly critical
of his behavior and leadership.

Earp, Wyatt (1848–1929) A "gunslinger," he had a varied career on each
side of the law. He is most remembered for the 30-second gunfight at
the O.K. Corral in 1881.

Geronimo (1829–1909) He was a
notorious Apache warrior who spent
30 years at war with settlers and
soldiers. He surrendered on three
different occasions.

Hickok, William (1837–1876) Famed as
a gunfighter, lawman, and gambler,
"Wild Bill" was recognized for
his long hair, twin pistols worn
backward, and short temper.

Joseph, Chief (1840–1904) A holy man
of the Nez Perce tribe, he is known
for his 1877 fighting retreat to
Canada, which won the admiration of
friends and foes.

Lewis, Meriwether (1774–1809)
Co-leader of the Lewis and Clark
expedition, he died mysteriously of
gunshot wounds.

Marshall, James Wilson (1810–1885)
An employee at John Sutter's mill in
California, he may have been the first
person to have discovered gold.

Portolá, Gaspar de (1716–1784) He was a
Spanish explorer and first governor of
New Spain (now California). Among
his settlements were San Diego and
San Francisco.

Santa Anna, Antonio Lopez de
(1794–1876) This Mexican president
and general destroyed the American
garrison at the Alamo. He called
himself the "Napoleon of the West."

Sheridan, Philip Henry (1831–1888)
Commanding General of the U. S.
Army in 1883, Sheridan is sadly
remembered for the remark, "The
only good Indian is a dead Indian."

Sherman, William Tecumseh
(1820–1891) He served as General of
the Army from 1869 to 1883. Under
his direction, 15 years of slaughtering
buffalo and Indians occurred.

Sitting Bull (1831–1890) A Sioux chief,
he directed the attack at the Little
Bighorn on Custer and his men.

Sutter, Johann Augustus (1803–1880)
He was operating a large agricultural
mill when gold was discovered
nearby. He is considered the father of
Sacramento, California.